Romeo Albert

BookLeaf
Publishing

India | USA | UK

19 Soft
Compulsions

Romeo Albert

BookLeaf
Publishing

Presentation by *BookLeaf Publishing*

Web: www.bookleafpub.com

E-mail: info@bookleafpub.com

Cover design by Eren Iusiumbeli

ISBN: 9789358314823

First edition 2024

DEDICATION

The 10th Poem in the Collection 'The Greek Mother Elephant' is a special dedication to my mum :)

ACKNOWLEDGEMENT

There are many people I need to thank for getting me where I am today. I need to first start with my mum and my sister who, not only have been through and unfathomable amount, but have also supported me in every single way while going through that, sacrificing a lot for me. I owe my mum everything, she is honestly the greatest mother in the world and has gone through too much for me to even understand. I love you, mum.

Next, I have some very important friends I need to thank. The Class of Miffmoffnskinny, my amazing English literature friends, I genuinely would not have been able to write nearly as many of the poems that I have without the love and support from you guys. Abi Deane, Annie Quayle, Kezia Cotterrell and Zarah Taylor, I love you all so much.

On the topic of English, I have teachers I need to thank too. The teachers from my secondary school who read my first ever novel and encouraged me to continue: Mr Earl, Miss Slinger, Mr Khawaja and Mr Wilson-Hughes, thank you.

To my English A Level teachers who pushed me even further: Mr Skinner, Miss Penn and Good old Moffen, thank you. I'd like to also make this book out to our late and most loving teacher at The BRIT School, Miss Elaine Nelson.

Finally, the boys who stuck with me through it all: Dylan Cray, Ash Down, Samuel Gurney and Alessio Genuardi. You're my boys. You've always been by my side and I will forever be by yours. Cheers for the encouragement for me to write this guys, thank you so much.

PREFACE

19 Soft Compulsions explores the following themes:
- Homophobia
- Christianity/Catholicism
- The Monarchy
- Sexism
- Sexual Assult/Rape
- Femicide
- Obsessive Compulsive Disorder
- Suicide
- Murder
- Transphobia
- Fetishization of Lesbians
- Friendship
- Love
- Domestic Violence
- Alcoholism
- Infidelity
- Heartbreak

Bleeding Berry

Nurtured fondly from seedling to tree
Oh kind berry, who wants to stomp on thee?
You are sure to have a wonderful destiny,
As from when you were a seed I saw your
purity.

You wept as I watered you in holy tears.
Cleared thine sins, cleared thine fears.
Your sweetness grew as many in the vine
Showed their pure nature, white, red, divine.

The leaves let you stain thy skin with ink.
But not an issue; it shows your creative think.
And too the leaves allowed thou to scream
foully with the heart,
Not a problem however, and sometimes leaves
would take part.

I watched you mature under mother leafs wing,
You stayed with her when she bled from her gap
for seedlings.
And so did thou father, who caressed her sweet
vine.
He told her thine blood is beautiful. Thine blood
is divine.

And so, sweet berry, I watch along with everyone else
How you matured into a fruit so heartfelt.
And despite your ink and swearing and living with woman blood,
To everyone else on the vine, oh how sweet berry you were loved.

Then, oh dear, came a time that we all thought forbid,
Sweet berry how could you clasp the heart of a something we thought we hid?
Son of God, please send your prayers, our dear berry is sick,
For another berry he found, the same sweet juice the berry lick.

Thou berry laboured every day, Saturday and sabbath,
All of which was praised, but this was surely havoc.
How could you go from caring, with open heart and mind
To doing something so not of this kind?

Ink, swearing, blood and working on the sun.
Retched berry that was okay, but now the leaves have no son.

We nurtured you from whence you were a tiny
little seed,
But since becoming this horrid fruit, I wish we'd
stomped on thee.

Queen Ana of Death

And so my head is light and yet I feel no weight
is lifted
As I watch my home fade, watch how my love
has drifted.
I sang to you every morning, sang a song of
English people
No matter how heavy their thighs, to mine eyes
they were equal.

A circle lies on both our fingers, yet you dent an
extra side,
With a hammer coated gold you sent one end so
wide,
So a triangle lays stuck on mine finger and on
yours.
The sharpened points cut me, and the soft sides
caress your pores.

And so, with this point digging deep into my
skin,
I start to bleed, I start to cry, fate begins to let
you win.
An angel chose this blood line many years ago.
You cut me out with the rusty prism on your
finger you bestow.

But now with God I stand, as I watch your heavy head,
Look down upon the children who can't even own a bed.
You reach down your hand, hold it out before their eyes,
Then in one quick swoop I watch you empty out their empty thighs.

For you. Yourself. The starving children give.
The homeless man gives to you his last means to live,
So you can grown happily, sprouting this holy love.
But old man, your mother is with me, dressed as white as a new born dove.

All the gold is yours, and you've kept this bloodline pure.
But I am with God now, and I don't think he's so sure.
So I asked that he let it rain, rain all over your reign,
Because remember, husband, that triangle you made will always remain.

Sigma Love

Listen closely to that melody,
That deafening yet gentle symphony.
Those waves traversing harsh beams in the air,
A star that spotlights 'the one' without care.

It's supposed to be peaceful, but it's often a
distraction,
A gravity that converts every feeling to
attraction,
A harmony that plays on loop in your mind
To remind you of the sweet, the gentle and kind.

The stars are aligning, my time just hasn't
arrived,
If the beacon shines again, I know I can survive.
Meanwhile, my emotions will rock gently on
this sea,
Acknowledge that he and her cannot always be
he and he.

Knocking on the same door makes the universe
scream,
The melody is shrieking; there's a better door it
seems.

There's an improved spotlight for all of us, so
don't get locked on the sun.
Soon, the universe will peacefully sing for you
and the one.

Vazo Timoria

With four arms and four legs lurking in his soul,
Young Harvey Miles stalked his pretty little
mole.
An elegant mistress who could flip, spin and
dance,
Little little Miles was not going to waste his
chance.

When she were all alone, venom spewing from
his gums,
Brutal Miles crept towards his prey oh so young.
The young dancers uniform was always kept
prestige;
Only the bite of this cruel insect could have it
tear and seize.

With one arm, it opened up her secure treasure
chest,
And then grabbed the innocent goods inside
before taking rest
Upon the ceiling with the mammal squealing
after attacked,
Then, grim Miles pounced down and broke her
innocent back.

With her goodness taken and all her loot tainted,
The performer wept, and exhaled 'dancing' once
before she fainted.
Her fate was destined never to dance a step
again,
The venom has left her spine incapable of mend.

Watching from above lies a creature of purple
glow.
His chest metallic grey, his eyes of Luna dismay,
Yet he was very sane and had a cricket of a
mind,
And after watching this absurdity, he knew of a
punishment as unkind.

His hands clasped a cylinder grey, and a capsule
on his spine
Allowed him to traverse down; this insect he
will find.
Mothers and fathers looked above and cried at
the glistening moon,
'Vazo Timoria, Vazo Timoria, don't take my
child so soon

He's been good and she's been grand' they cried,
But their words meant little to him.
This Demi of Punishment with one look tried,
And found the beast of sin.

'Little little Harvey Miles, look how you dance.
You dance the world into a deceitful little trance.
I saw what you did. I know who you are.
You may be loved. "Best dancer of the year"But
from that title you are far.'

The creature of purple appeared before Miles in
glowing violet,
He whispered words unknown to us, except for
one: 'violence'.
'You hurt an innocent creature, yet the world
proceeds to turn?
Oh little Harvey Miles, I think it's time you
learned.'

With the shudder of his deep voice no longer in
an echo,
The being made a puppet of Miles, made him
float and bellow.
'Vazo Timoria, Miles, your fate is now aligned,
For I'm going to take what you once robbed:
your pretty little spine.'

Harvey Miles screamed, and ratty vultures flew
the air.
Their claws in handcuffs, echoing any scream
Miles snared.
Like a thick wooden puzzle, each vertebrae
knocked out of line.

'The world will be in pieces when they know
how you truly shine.'

Seizing in pain, Miles shook and bled onto the
ground.
'He will live' the creature muttered, and turned
his form around.
Below him, in a wheelchair, lied the girl Harvey
once hurt.
'I'm sorry I can't fix you' he cried 'but know he
is now the one to lie in the dirt.

Like a fire rose, your heart will heal and you will
soon be loved.
With no rose and only fire will he burn to dust.
Let him live his life defending vultures; he can
no longer cause harm.
But you, young one, you can heal in the comfort
of our arms.'

The Blind Eyes of Union Crossing

Welcome to this wondrous town of nature and
delight,
Filled with anything you could ever possibly
want within your sight,
A cathedral mountains tall, and parks and fields
and schools,
Anything you want is here, and your eyes can
see them all.

Many live here in the heart of England's lovely
Union Crossing,
Oh what wonderful families to gaze upon:
Easter, Christmas or boxing!
I promise they can't miss you, their eyes see
everything,
And their ears are tuned to hear even the
dimmest, darkest ding!

So, of course, it's understandable that their eyes
can spot a tear
In the great painting of Union Crossing that all
union eyes bear.
These friendly folk would surely spot some
misfits in the crevice

Of their lovely homely town that offers such
wholesome friendly service.

Vultures fly high above each and every soul,
They don't feel the need to hide, they've
achieved their main goal
Of having claws so sharp they frighten away any
form of care
To any harm done in Union Crossing's nightly
air.

So every night a vulture or two will spot a lonely
deer,
Walking her beautiful antlers through the starry
Union air,
And they will swoop and tug and tear at her
gracious skin,
While she pleads within the ears of passing
Union kin.

Their eyes are wide, they see all, every single
tear,
The cutting of her throat and the tugging of her
hair,
They watch the violence occur on their lovely,
united streets,
And swiftly brisk their eyes away from any
bleeding meat.

They hear and see but choose to believe no
crime is taking place,
They ignore the vultures tearing through evening
deers poor face,
Some will smile all the while this indecency
occurs,
And walk away, and pretend that may haps their
eye is blurred.

And so a deer is left to rot when the vultures
bidding's done.
Her screams of agony put to hold until the rising
sun
Can guide her out the crevices of Union
Crossing's bone,
And she limps an injured journey, lost, hurt and
alone.

Welcome, young deers, all of you, to lovely
Union Crossing,
Your screams and cheers, we will hear, Easter,
Christmas or boxing!
So take a ride over, and enjoy a lovely, blissful
time.
We promise, if anything happens, we will see it
with our pure eyes.

Keep smiling, my dears. We love to see you
smile.

The Daughter of Aphrodite

Sprinkled with the pink of Cupid's delight
And sparkled with Herculean strength and the
like,
A young and beautiful pearl emerged in our
society,
Fresh from a holy Oyster laid the daughter of
Aphrodite.

Virgin born, but confidence riddled,
Her hierarchy doubled then tripled,
And from the grass she plucked a stem
Which she whispered into both flute and gem.

A harmonious gift the goddess made,
Removed the serpent from the flower and on the
serpent played
A wondrous tune no Adonis can avoid,
As she welcomed every eloped girl and boy.

This melody and tune, corrupted with fangs
Lured citizens to raise her crown to a land
Of talent and purity, where everyone there
cheers
Screams of joy and happy futures for their peers.

So surrounded by friends and bleeding
polygamy,
This beautiful pearl ensured her holy history
As goddess of beauty, talent and lust.
Oh their happiness she gained. Their happiness
and trust.

Aphrodite's young pearl had lulled into their
minds.
Her voice and beauty enough to blur their eyes
to kind.
And unbeknownst to her, the largest mice to
which she sung,
Was the God's finest Astraea, the biggest prize
she had won.

Another deity on this troubled, liquid, mossy
stone,
But this young pearl saw no threat; her trust in
pearl had grown.
So with slithered night and thoughts of scales
there should be no harm,
As these thoughts remain well hidden behind
pearl's beauty love and arms.

With trust obtained, pearl whispered for Astraea
to be honest.
So on a holy iris, Astraea sang of her most
desired Adonis.

She harmonised so carelessly, spilling the secret
of who she loved,
And the daughter of Aphrodite had now planted
her hidden dove.

The following season, this slimy pearl sought
out this well spoken prince,
Knowing that another god was desperately in
love with it,
And with trust obtained she lead him to
Astraea's holy home,
Where they both sang sweet nothings into
Astraea's heart shaped dome.

Astraea, alone, heard and wept at the songs of
her two lovers.
One who's trust she had given and the one she
hoped discovered
That they were meant to love one another, it was
carved into the sky,
But a Lamia had arrived and slurped up every
starry fly.

Left in tears Astraea fled back up the holy
mountains,
She wept so much the sun became a moon of
cyan fountains
At the thought of an unfortunately desirable,
beautiful creature

Deflowering the one thing she whispered with trust and her hearts feature.

When pearl was done, her mother looked down with utter shame.
She watched her creature of beauty become reptilian without tame.
And out of fear of losing all she once lulled to be her friends,
She made a vulture of this young Adonis, his future she endeavoured to end.

She looked around her hoard of once acquired gems
Of people who looked up to her, people who thought she was a friend,
And no matter how hard pearl tried to play her serpent flute,
Only the tears of an alligator spat out, and not a soul was amused.

So pearl was left to cry at the shame of what she'd lost.
Not the shame of what she's done, she only cared about the cost.
Her beauty and lust could no longer grant her liberty,
As every soul surrounding her now only sees her serpent ability.

The Wasp of Immorality

Across the holy mountains lie Gods of Love and
Mayhem,
Beings of heart and chaos that blossom all veiny
stems
Of humanities greatest motions and all of which
they feel.
They gave them the ability to love, to be hurt
and to heal.

Duality, yes, but these creatures truly create
unworldly traits!
Every emotion that you feel bleeds from their
potent states.
And it's the mix of love and chaos that truly
sprouts who we are.
Uniqueness is inevitable to those born from
conflicting stars.

But with such goodness pumped into the souls
of innocent kin,
The mountains have in waste a pile of discarded
sin,
And while some of it is sprinkled into the yin
and yang of humanity,

The overbearing wastage is left to shiver beyond
sanity.

And sanity it had, as all emotions do.
That which can feel can grow a body too.
So laced in needles and spikes to remind us of
our mortality,
This pile of fear took an insect form: The Wasp
of Immorality.

It's hornet fur is dreaded in all unwanted
thoughts,
Anything remotely bad flows through its venom
and inner warts.
It's wet, clear wings can flap as loud as one's
inner voice
Screeching affirmations of harm; worry without
choice.

Oh, and how its lethal stinger was so large one
doesn't know.
Half the size of this wasps body, and its body
was not low.
It was born from human sin, so a human size it
has.
And half of it is this silver razor of a mentally
crippling mass.

But surely an Hymenoptera so large would go
noticed?
Surely it would be slain or imprisoned by the
being closest?
And if, oh dear, it were to somehow come to
humanity's little rock,
Surely they'd find and fright it away through
their selfish mental shock?

Oh if only it would have been as convenient as
this.
This glowing wasp of slimy blue had a trick to
stalk down missed.
Into the vapour of the air, this insect turned to
mist,
And plummeted down in a predatory stream, a
cloudy foggy fist.

Upon the mortal rock of water, life and leaf,
Lie beings of time who thrive on both happiness
and belief
That they will provide kindness to those who
require,
That that will deliver good memories before they
expire.

Humanity has many breeds; adolescents are only
one.

And all male adolescents receive a gift on the
rise of their fourteenth sun,
That opens up their minds to the world of
creating young.
Arousal is an early emotion for the adolescent
son.

Early yet natural, and perfectly sane!
As a teen grows older these emotions do the
same
And maturity develops alongside kindness and
innocence.
Preparation for adulthood, no fear, just
happiness.

So joy and pleasure and selfless and kind,
Are all wired deep in a humans design,
And they are built to care for all those they
surround,
Empathy exists in many; in young hearts it
should be found.

A happy ending, correct? Most teenagers built to
love!
Empathy in a good man's heart should help him
feel like a dove:
Free from distress and laced in certainty;
absolutely nothing to fear!

There's no such thing as anxiety when you don't
have an insect in your ear.

But unfortunately for one, an insect is on his
way.
A boy filled with empathy and care for all that
may
Cross his lonely path, which he greets with a
happy smile.
Worryless is the boy, for there's nothing to fear
for a while!

The Wasp of Immorality sniffs out the fourteenth
sun.
In a gaseous form, it tracks the arrival of the new
adolescent in the run.
This happy boy is greeted with the emotions of
life,
And the wasp is ready to feast… carve the meat
with its stinger of a knife.

Happy Birthday, teenage boy, for its time for you
to grow!
Candles on his cake combust with a hefty, happy
blow,
And in the mist of the smoke, the vapoured wasp
takes its chance.
A predator on prey, it leaps without a stance.

Disguised in the air, it swoops into the boys
eyes,
Beats within his heart, and shoots through the
ties
Of his veins and his organs as it locates the
mind,
And takes rest upon the spot that helps the boy
unwind.

His mind overtaken, the boy feels a sense of
dread.
What happened to the happiness that everyone
once said
Would arrive as he aged into happy teenage
years,
Filled with laughter and carelessness amongst
him and his peers?

No. An unfathomable sense that his mind is off
Floods him to the brim as his emotions feel less
soft.
Something is creepily wrong, he feels his mind
growing cysts.
Unwelcome thoughts are blooming, an intruder
feels amidst.

He tries to brush it off and he turns to his mother
for hugs,

The wasp felt this moment of love, it shivered and it shrugged,
And it punched its stinger into the brain where the boys heart lines left.
His mother asked what he wished for, and his brain whispered 'her death'.

But that wasn't right! That's not what he wants at all!
He repelled from the hug in fear, and felt the need to ball.
The wasp had its first meal, and oh how relieved it felt.
Enjoying the meal of empathy and fear as the tastes together melt.

Our poor boy fled to his room, fearing his own mind.
How on earth could his skull brew something so unkind?
And I wish this was all, but we'd only just begun.
The boy feels an impending inevitability that this won't be the last time he's stung...

And thus the wasp grew larger in the comfort of his brain,
Paralysing the boy with unwanted thoughts and feasting on what remained.

Intruding every lovable action with dreadful
thoughts of harm,
And slurping on the empathy that floods from
the boys left arm.

He would no longer hold a knife out of fear he'd
cut a soul,
And in big crowds his brain would spit 'you
want a bomb to blow here a hole!'
And even though he knows this isn't what he'd
like,
The wasp continues to eat his fear, learning new
recipes for it to spike.

And soon it found a brand new toy that it could
definitely play,
The boys new found arousal was hidden out of
the wasps way,
But now it can smell it, and what a time it could
have.
How can a wasp ensure arousal drives our poor
boy mad?

Immorality is its blood. It takes whats right and
makes it wrong.
So with a disoriented buzz, and lethal sting, the
wasp deludes a song,
Reshaping the perspective on the boys
untouched attraction,

Presenting it as distasteful and convinces him he loves disgusting actions.

For it is right to love adults, and people your age resemble,
But the melodious venom tricks the boy; 'your lust is in the younger assemble',
And quickly fear arose, and not to the wasps surprise,
A phobia of the youth soon began to arise.

Being around infants flooded his brain with bile,
The venom is thick and clogging, and makes him think of things most vile,
The wasp nearly has full control, for every approach of a child,
Caused the boy to almost feel aroused, and this feeling sent him wild.

He ran away and hid, this had gone too far,
For first they were just thoughts, but now emotions are on par.
He knows his brain is wrong, but can you argue with emotion?
Is it possible for the wasp to truly alter feelings in motion?

Well, good friends, yes. Yes it sadly is.

The wasps hallucinogenic stinger has shrouded
the brain in mist.
And his true attraction is hidden behind a
charade of bile and shadows,
His true arousal now a puppet on the strings of
the wasps immoral hallows.

And the boy could not shake urges as well as he
could thoughts.
Urges feel to real, and his groin the stinger
sought
To send some final venom, to truly strengthen
the illusion,
Make the boy belief these sexual desires are not
indeed delusion.

And so the bidding's done, and the wasp
proceeds to feed.
The boy worries so much that he will spread his
seed
On someone who won't allow, someone who
won't consent,
He truly believes he's a vulture crossing sent.

Every female he befriends, he fears he will
scratch.
Violate in ways that cannot go unmatched. And
as for children, well the boy always averts his
gaze

Out of fear that he will do something... well
something that won't amaze.

Oh I can't bare to utter it. They are too
disgusting.
He avoids all women and children for a vulture
is a must thing!
What else could he be, his feelings are too real!
Oh but if only he knew of the wasp! His life
back we could steal...

It has grown too strong. The poison overflowing.
It's flooded him so much, he's no longer
growing.
The boy has been paralysed by his fear of
immorality,
And thus the wasp reminds the boy of his
limited mortality.

He didn't want to hurt anyone, so he made sure
he won't.
The wasp released its blade of a stinger out onto
the moat
Of the boys flooded arms of worry, bile and
tears,
A leg long blade of injustice, laced in all his
fears.

So the boy took this razor, and he unclogged all his blood,
Let the venom that once intruded his mind release into the flood.
Out of his wrists, the illusion slowly poured,
As the boy was left to rot, killed while he could still be mourned...

It is a tale that will always make loved ones weep in pain,
For of course he was not evil, the young boy died in vein.
He was always going to be mourned, his thoughts and urges were not him.
It was The Wasp of Immorality that made him believe he was to sin.

As for this retched wasp, well he had his final feast,
Before laying his wrongful eggs into our trees and yeast
Spreading the intrusive plague among many girls and boys,
The Wasps of Immorality now play with many emotional toys.

Help them... They don't know they deserve it.
But they do.

The Contamination Worm

Sinful larvae squirming in the ground,
Born from anxiety of the Wasps' gruesome and
profound
And grimly deposited faecal remnant:
Meet the gruesome parasites of the Wasps'
unholy element.

Arriving in grille groups, short and white,
Like an intestinal rubber ball that was thrown up
by light,
For not even the stars want to touch this
disgusting ball of germs,
All souls are ignorant to the Wasp's
Contamination Worm.

Unlike the flightful insect, the worm doesnt need
patience,
It can begin its possessing journey from any
toddler vacant,
For a mind that's yet to be moulded is a mind
ripe for hosting,
As The Contamination Worm hunts; a toddler
requires its dosing.

Ahh, an infant found, and their mind has much
to grow,
Plenty of room for the worm to make a vile
home,
So it wiggles up her harm and slithers within her
food,
The parasite simply requires the human to be in
a hungry mood.

Starvation indeed it has, as all young toddlers
do,
The girls immature spaghetti, sat awaiting an
impatient goo,
Watches as the girl thrusts deep her lumpy hands
As she slurps up the grey wastage of the worm,
as it planned.

Her food went down her throat, but the beast slid
up her nose,
Causing her twitch and gag and clench tight her
eyes and toes.
It curl around her brain, sticky and laced in
phlegm,
Resembling a faecal and organ covered stem.

The Worm now feeds on a more specific fear,
Intoxicating the girl to feel that anything she
steps near

Is infused with diseases and eggs and all things
fungal,
Oh, the vile parasite turned her brain into a
nested, pubic jungle.

Whenever she boards a train, the girl behind an
exam,
Upon ever questionable stain that remains
unknown to man,
And sometimes she'll refuse to sit down all
together,
Standing is better than the risk of her rear
contaminated forever.

Oh, heaven forbid she walk near a pile of waste,
Excrement from a dog is a enough to make her
bleach her face,
And the worm just sits and feeds, loving her
every fear,
A germaphobes life induced by the worm in her
ear.

'Wash and wash and wash' the worm whispers
for her to clean
For the more hygienic her body, the more the
worm can lean
Deeper into her mind, slide easily to her skull,
All control to the worm, all human control
annulled.

The girl finds herself curled in cycles of
bleaching her poor hands,
Causing them to crack and bleed till their bluer
than if a band
Was to be strapped on her wrist, cutting off all
life supply,
She's ending her life! And she doesn't know!
The worm has laced in her lies.

Stuck in the shower for hours at a time,
Scared her oyster is riddled in a white fungus
full of grime
Or that the brown pile she stepped ever so near,
Has delivered intestinal parasites to her stomach
through her ear.

Her immune system is fried, it's sizzled beyond
repair,
She'll decompose soon, and the worm will resell
from her hair
And find a brand new host as the germaphobe
dies,
After embedding her in such grim little lies.

The girl never found love, for she was too scared
to kiss,
Any opportunity to reproduce or to have any
kids,

Was lost due to fear of giving her partner a disease,
She even debated slicing off her oyster, just to keep any partner clean

She did not want to infect anyone.
And due to that she had no daughter or son.
The poor girl didn't have a chance to ever become a wife
Because the worm halted her ability to go outside and experience life.

Ripples of Care

A phantom recently took over my skin,
And those lyrics it made me think I thought I'd
keep within,
I never wanted to let the juices of the mind
Be briefly limited to something of this usual
kind.

But this ghost has a firm grasp, and perhaps to
let it go
I must first sing the song of every word it show.
Oh, and a song it had, one id never heard before.
Culturing me in the music of man's internal war.

While this ghost reminds me of the melody that
soon all will be healed,
For some reason this gaping wound is far from
being sealed.
I am yet to believe I've resorted to using my
thumbs for this,
But I suppose the ghost won't let go until I
whisper of your bliss.

Indecision is a plague, yet somehow can't be
caught.

But this phantom on my left hand has truly left
me taught
That sometimes we hear the universe sing just
for a little while,
And when the song is done we sit and wait for
the lyrics. The same smile.

But there's supposed to be something better, the
reason for my words held back.
The universe is lulling me down another
cheerful track.
But on this journey all I can think is the
happiness you gave me before.
Our eyes were locked for one night, and now I
am left sore.

And I wish that hell had sent you here, like all
sweet berries are.
I wish I could call you evil, wish it was your
fault for my scar.
But sweet is the name of the berry, and
beautifully sweet you are.
I sure hope the universe has saved for me a
fruitful bleeding star.

I shouldn't do this, yet I will, tell you all that's
on my mind.
Knowing you won't hear this song, knowing
your heart it won't find.

I should just follow the music, locate the better
door
Before the universe has to screech, before before
and before.

I'm sorry that one night had me hooked to your
gorgeous smile,
I'm sorry the way your stared at me made my
eyes the river Nile,
I don't understand how the universe can sing us
together so fast,
Then after one sweet taste of the berry, make it
no longer last?

I've never had a conversation flow like a song
before you.
I shouldn't tell you that your jokes and presence
made me laugh too.
I shouldn't go against the universe's song, the
melody of love.
But as much as I don't want to care, my problem
is I care too much.

I know you don't like I do, and that will always
be okay.
The song is for everyone, a better a path for you
the melody too lay.
And if I'm not in those lyrics, then you shouldn't
be in mine.

But before I stop singing, let me rhyme one last time.

Thank you for showing me how to break the dam of the male brain.
The dam built by raising, the dam of brutal tame.
For centuries the gods and vines had it sealed like a vault.
But when my heart was torn, too the dam shattered without halt.

So thank you for letting me feel, I never thought I could.
Thank you for the waves that never I thought I would
Bare to see again until the end of our stone.
I suppose the universe needs me to grow and listen alone.

I want to find you again, or for you to find me.
In these waves of emotion and harmony, somewhere in this sea.
I hate letting go of the fun we could have had.
The universe connected us through every star, and when our hands held it became a fad.

If I was the right person, the wrong time wouldn't matter.

I wouldn't be here waiting with a heart filled
with shatter.
But I want you to be right, as much as I
shouldn't.
Thank you for bringing flesh back to a brain
once wooden.

I'll miss your wonderful smile, I'll miss the way
you laugh.
I'll miss the jokes you made and the hugs of the
warmest baths.
I'll miss the way that we spoke on any airy site,
How our timeless conversations were never dead
by daylight.

I've never had a kiss mean as much as yours,
Never had a touch leave my hairs standing on
pores,
And I want to feel it again, feel your presence on
my hair,
Put my nose to yours and give in to the nightly
air.

I want to hug you tight on every single star,
Whisper to every soul just how beautiful and
sweet you are.
I've kissed and hugged different forms of souls
before

But you were different. You were loving,
wonderful and raw.

But that's not now. And May never be.
I just don't understand how it feels like we've
known each other an eternity.

Soon I must depart to my new favourite door.
The universe is blissful, and sings like it did
once before.
The phantom that has me clutched makes me
shiver at the thought,
But the relaxing tingles must soon mean that
happiness will soon be sought.

The Greek Mother Elephant

In the warm beaches of Cyprus lies a mother
with a heart
So large all other mammals can hear it beat
through the sandy parts
Of the Cypriot shores, where there she did give
birth
To two small Greek elephants who she will
cherish on this earth.

Being the lovely mother she is, she sacrificed
all,
To ensure that her poor babies will grow with
trunks so tall
That they can achieve anything their little snouty
hearts desire,
For within this mothers belly is a roaring,
loving, Greek fire.

But she must raise these two silver presents all
alone,
For the father often shrouds his trunk in a fungal
liquid unknown,
Slurping and slurring his elephant mind into a
delusional, toxic fountain,

Where his entire brain melts a lazy river down
Cypriot mountains.

This elephant is strong, and has a leech-filled
soul.
All the love drained, and replaced with the liquid
coal
Of the sinful juice he snorts up his slurry trunk,
Leaving him dazed and immobile, the mother
must also tend to this drunk.

But sometimes he loses all blood, loses all
loving feels,
And throws the nearest branch at the mother so
unhealed,
All the while she stands there, shielding her
innocent young,
As they listen this forceful beast scream
unworldly tongues.

The mother does not eat, the priority is her
babies,
The father elephant yells and steals her food that
just maybe
Would have been enough to give her some more
added strength,
But she won't eat if it means her children have
food in arms length.

The Greek Mother is growing frail, she cannot
tend for all.
She's been strong for 18 years, but 18 years to
stall.
Her eldest elephant tries to defend against the
beast,
He doesn't steal food from him now he's older
and has learned how to speak.

The drunken creature leaves, then comes back
leaves again,
Each time the children cry less and less in their
Cypriot den,
For now they want him gone, they prey for him
to go,
The mother will do better if raising her kids was
a solo show.

And what a show it was, for the elephants loved
to dance!
But the father remembers none of it, as he foams
and foul prance
Of liquid fungal teeth, emerging from his nose,
The elephants want their dad to watch them sing,
but now they hope he goes.

For he is never here, just a burden and presence,
Drinking away his life and his children
encourage an entrance

For a way for him to stop! Despite all he has
done!
They still care for him, so please dad, care for
your son.

The 11:11 Genie

Twice a day a personal genie arrives from
beneath the heavenly skies,
And mid amongst our clocks does it take
disguise,
So we never see it, but our hearts are
conditioned to know,
That this wish fulfilling creature at 11:11 will
show.

But people have slotted this genie onto strings.
This invisible tradition now a salve forever to
bring,
Utterly cruel tricks onto our generations youth,
Threatening their futures with the imprisoned
genies false truth.

So these puppeteer guards begin to drain the
creature dry,
Rinsing it's fairytale of cruel unfathomable lies,
Camouflaging them in music and heart shaped
paper taps,
Promising young children lucky directions on
life's map.

All they have to do, is listen to their song,

Share it with their loved ones so they can sing
along,
And they must greet the song with praise, ensure
they have it claimed,
Plus they must all punch the paper hearts to rip
away bad days.

But this is where the guards begin to make it
sour,
For they threaten that if children don't do this,
then at some future hour,
Their lives will suffer greatly, they'll lose
careers, loved ones and joy,
So many children share the songs of the
imprisoned genies toy.

Traditions are growing bitter, and profitable they
are too,
For each time they sing these songs, the
puppeteer guards earn a pound or two.
So I'm here to tell you dearly now, these songs
are full of lies.
If you chose not to share it, you won't suffer a
terrible demise

They've taken something pure and have tricked
many a soul.
And those with wasps in their mind are their
targeted goal,

How dare you all think it's sane to trick the
children of this planet
Into thinking they won't have a life if the hearts
aren't punched till the white is vanished.

I assure you all, dear children, your futures
aren't at risk,
Keep scrolling through your day and don't
worry about their music disc,
For if we all relax and stop singing their
melodies so cursed,
The genie will be free, and 11:11 will be a happy
verse.

'A Cat in The Rain :)'

My friend told me to write poem wholesome and
light hearted,
'A Cat in The Rain' he said as his lips slowly
parted
A heart warming smile in the hopes that I might
write
Something that isn't gory or tragic, something
that's happy and bright!

He wants me, for once, to write something that's
normal,
But fuck that, I'm unique! This poem is not
going to be formal!
So you want 'A Cat in The Rain'; there's so
much I can twist in that,
For how can I craft a dreaded and gnarly
outcome for this poor innocent cat?

Gore isn't the only option, for 'a cat' can be
yonic,
And 'the rain' can be the pleasurable urge that is
the female tonic
Flooding the mind with hormones, dazing her in
desire.

Or, perhaps an oxymoron I can make with rain
and align it with fire.

What if perhaps the cat is falling several stories
from a star?
Plummeting away from a sizzling ball as it
travels dreadfully far?
This poem could be a test for the theory of nine
lives.
Will a cat always land on its feet if it's falling an
unfathomable size?

Backtracking to the imagery that embraced that
which is feminine,
'A Cat in The Rain' could be a tail about the
perversion from deep within
Our heteronormative society, lesbian
fetishisation:
How indeed it's perverted to watch two felines
embrace their wetness in todays nation.

There's so much you can tell, and oh golly am I
insane.
But all good poets are! I'm not the only one to
blame!
I'm not gonna just write a wholesome tail of a
cat alone on soggy streets!
What's the deal with that? How will that make
ends meet?

Don't be afraid to be grotesque, kill the cat in
acid rain.
Drown it and scorch it, but don't let it die in
vein,
The sizzling of a feline, stripped away in water
Has a greater story to tell of a lonely, abandoned
daughter…

For you see, there was, in fact, a cat: a feline left
alone,
Booted out of the house, for promiscuity it must
atone.
It was shamed for giving birth; getting pregnant
in its home,
Now it's left to walk beneath a storm, where
hungry foxes roam…

Watching this poor feline cough a unpurred
song,
Waiting for her to be drenched in the wetness
forgotten long,
And when indeed, she is covered in a fury coat
of liquid,
The foxes will seize their pray, as the blood
sucking tic did.

The cat scurried away trying to hide from
nocturnal eyes,

Watching her every move, watching her try to
disguise,
But another cat emerged, and to the foxes'
surprise,
The two felines converged and embraced their
wetness combined.

For they were not sent to be the meal of a male
fox,
They were crafted by the deities to caress each
others locks,
And gruesomely the mammals, drooling,
ravaged and starved,
Sat hungrily staring at the two young girls
explore their curves and carves.

They enjoyed it thusly. Enjoyed it too much. The
all released a grizzly moan as their bodies went
untouched,
But they enjoyed a show, hidden amongst dark,
Watching the felines merge, they released a
snarly bark.

When the show had ended, and with no tickets
for sale,
The foxes who snuck in to watch raised their
puffy tails,
And pounced out from the bushes to enjoy their
long teased feast,

The poor felines were always food for the foxes
come to meet…

The 13th Creature

Superstition is a monster, and meet number 13,
An emulation of organs and clovers with a blood
leakage frightfully seen
Spewing across the drain-piped floors,
You better check atleast three times that you
locked your wooden doors…

It's birth was boiled after an hotel room
overheat,
A blaze did strike and burned alive the poor
souls of burning meat.
Their swirly bodies on the floor thirteen crawled
together into one,
And thus was born The 13th Creature, an
abominable unholy son.

It's had four stomachs in need of filling,
So it turned to a mirror and gave a brutal
drilling,
With a twisted spin of femurs and teeth,
It cracked open the mirror and on the glass did it
feast.

It's face now sharpened and stomachs lined with
grate,

The 13th Creature began its quest of hate,
Where it would fulfil its most unholy fate,
And it began by seeping beneath a sewage grate.

The poor innocent children who walked among
the drain,
Their ankles were struck and pulled beneath and
feasted on in pain;
With 6 children surgically and dominantly
consumed,
The 13th Creature swam the sewers to find
where else it could be bemused.

Ahh… a staircase oh so thin, the perfect place to
hide.
Whenever a couple would cross, attending
alternate sides,
Both of them would fall into the hands of the
beast!
The delectable nature of unlucky humans is such
a to die for treat.

So like a hotel, this floor will not be counted,
Skip the 13th poem if your superstition has you
doubted,
And thus the following tail jumps from twelve to
fourteen,
If you choose to have this poem left unseen…

An Oopsie Whoopsie Bleeding Tail

Good Evening boys and girls and welcome to
our wondrous Christmas Tail!
Oh do I have journey in store for you, and we're
about to set sail.

Don't be fooled by who I am, for Saint Nick I
am not.
Leviticus is my name, Saint Nick's a friend I've
long had got.

So sit back and relax, for our stories about to
shed
It's time I introduce you to our Holy Boy, Bled.

Ho Ho So, Little Bled met a boy who he tried to
make a friend
But this boy often played dress up, to be a girl
he'd pretend
But on the nice list Bled remain's for he stripped
away his disease
Playing dress up for this man has now come to
cease.

He's just obeying his leaders! He's doing what
he's told.
He's raised for all genders to remain as they are
till they grow old!
So even if it causes them insanity and self-harm
immense,
A man is a man and a woman is a woman…
that's just common sense!

But this is not the only good deed Bled has done
For one morning his sister announced the
planned death of her son
And Bled, of course, being so good, put an end
to child killings
He forced his sister into labour, unfilled her
fillings.

Poor little Bled, his sister died in birth!
But sacrifices must be made to put a new child
on the earth,
Aww, don't cry Bled, you're doing the right
thing,
A woman's life is worth less than the cells her
uterus bring.

Chocolate embedded with toys, that indeed is
too far!
As for children's lives ended in school? Mere
detention that's on par.

It's logistical to support life while it's in the womb,
But in institutions it's a free for all for whoever can escape the room.

Prancer The Reindeer

Tis the festive season, a season built to give!
A time to find out inner selflessness and enjoy
our time to live.
And when the snow has bedded our streets in
blankets white,
We know jolly times await us, and the future
indeed is bright!

Upon a snowy hill in Britain's land of wonder,
Beneath the icy duvets and sky cymbals of
thunder,
An old man, wheelchair bed, lies alone on
Christmas eve,
His only winter joy brought by his hidden gifts
beneath his sleeve.

For you see he has a heart, plastic built like all
his rest,
And he wears it open to prove to the world he
indeed is doing his best,
To bring joy to the children in his small, royal
town,
As he lives patiently alone in his festive, cotton
gown.

But, oh, why was he left all by himself?
No family, no friends, only a mere elf on his shelf.
It does indeed feel natural to show the poor man pity.
He makes wondrous mascots for children, yet he's alone in this city.

You see, young winter friends, this old man was left to rot to the side.
For when he was younger, his own wife sought what the old man could not provide.
Being numb from below the lungs, half his body is icy cold,
His sexual desire aged and withered, half of him is old.

So satisfaction was the one present the old man couldn't gift,
So his old wife took to receive a distasteful helping lift
From someone he resembles but can indeed do the job.
His wife and own brother made a slippery beast behind frozen door knobs.

And, oh, the heartbreak felt when the old man discovered,

That his own wife and brother had become each
others lovers.
For she had pranced away with many men that
eve,
Compensating for a year of feeling beastly
displease.

Half his body numb, the old man did his worst,
For vengeance is a liquid that will quench the
coldest thirst,
And with his skills in mascot making, and giant
puppet elves,
The old man remained awake for many moons
and many twelves.

He rolled around outside and hid beneath the
trees,
And shot the festive horse of Father Christmas'
many breeds.
He then proceeded to skin this lonely reindeer
alive,
For a mascot will be made with this collected
Hyde.

On Christmas Day he pleaded beneath his frozen
phone,
That his old brother and his new lover would not
leave him alone,

And out of bitter pity and a subtle show of
sympathy,
They listened to the man's cold Christmas
symphony.

Driving up the winters mountains, passing all
the festive lands,
And all Christmas fairs, and ice cream drenched
vans,
The couple met the man for a holy Christmas'
dinner.
He invited them both in, biting his tongue as not
to yell 'sinner'.

The meat they ate resembled rubber, a feast
unhad before.
The gravy was was laced in ice cubes, oh how
the man was poor.
Indeed he couldn't afford a wholesome
Christmas turkey,
But what was this meat that was left to taste so
murky?

The feast's besides the point, for the point is
they were here,
The two of them together within the cold man's
ear.
Left beside a heart they once had left to numb,

'Please follow me to my bedroom when your
Christmas meal is done.'

He had made them a present! Oh how generous
is he!
They began to actually feel dreadful about the
cunts they once did be.
So, curious, they followed to see what the man
had made.
He was an expert in making elves, perhaps that
was the gift he was to gave?

When they approached his room, ahh yes, an elf
was wooden crafted!
Rather large this one was, but from the old man
this was hearted,
For he had made mascot elves once larger than a
shed!
But this one seemed to match his brother from
his green toes to festive head.

'Oh, dear brother… an elf of me did you so
kindly make?'
Whispered the old man's sibling as he glanced at
his sweet, resembled fake.
'Ahh, yes my old friend, a new invention I have
here got!
It will resemble you in every way, not inch left
to not!'

Feeling sorry for the man, the wife almost wept
a tear,
She left him and now guilt floods her as well as
a newfound fear
As to how she could be so cruel! How could she
leave the innocent bloke?
Ahh... Innocence is fascinating when
perspective is misspoke...

An odour began to penetrate central holes to the
brain,
And the ex wife looked down to see a red and
vile stain,
So she followed it behind the bed where
gruesomely there hid
Was a sliced and gutted reindeer, oh heaven
forbid!

Before the wife could scream, a cane whacked
behind her skull,
And the old man's brother vision blurred and he
collapsed upon a bowl
Of metal and wood left behind the old man's
broken legs,
Then the man used his sculpting tools to make a
mascot from his new pegs,

For to piece his sculpture together, he needs a
skeleton thick,
Lucky for him, asleep and conscious is his
special little trick.
He must first sew together the inner puppets
workings,
So he can be the first to make a mascot
responsive, breathing, lurking.

He stripped off the clothing of his family's
Christmas cheer,
And he began his work on the lower half of the
butchered reindeer,
Where, drug induced, he chopped away his old
wife's feet and hands,
And upon the stubs he sewed hooves so on four
his wife could stand.

Then upon her spine he made a minor incision,
Two small holes, carefully measured, oh the old
man makes cruel decisions.
Like the gnarly centipede that once riddled our
young minds,
The old man slotted his brother upon his wife's
behind.

One hole had a tube cluttered into her lower
bowles,

And he slotted that tube into the rectum of his
brother so profound.
The other holes circumference was cruelly
measured to match
That of the brothers weapon for making the
beast with two back.

And the beast he made, for he sewed them in
position.
The horror on their faces was the old man's only
inquisition.
But he knew for his justice, he'd have to
sacrifice that fate,
For in order to make this mascot, he'd have to
seal both their face.

The carcass of the mammal is now ready for use,
With a needle and thread he sewed his wife
within the reindeers juice.
The only skin left to show was that of her back,
Where her new found lover laid stitched with his
stem grossly sewn black.

The wooden pieces of the elf slotted perfectly on
his brother,
And the end result resembled a mascot built to
look like no other!
For on the outside it was a statue of an elf riding
a deer,

But on the inside laid the sleeping puppets of his family oh so dear.

Two last things left to do before it's ready to sell.
He pushed his hands through both mouth pieces to ensure they'd never tell.
So with a knife he sliced off both their hidden tongues,
And injected them with medication so infection wouldn't leave them done.

Soon the couple awoke, agony settling in,
And he heard their desperate screams come from within,
But on the festive coating, the screams resembled roars
Of a deer and a cheer in the forest of snowy floors.

'Prance for me, old friends, prance like you did that night!
Show me the infidelity that sews you both so tight!
And do not even attempt to ever stop your dance,
For a furnace inside I have equipped, and you do not want that chance!

If I ever see you do what you were not for
tamed!
A simple button press will erupt you both in
flames,
And a slow death you'll have as this winter
comes to cease,
Now tis the season of giving! So from my hands
you're released!'

To the highest bidder, the mascot was then sold,
The rich man was pulled aside, and the old man
then told,
'Keep the mascot in your garden, where I can
watch it play,
For if it's ever to stop working, I know how to
make it stay.

Give it a poke and a thrash, abuse it with a whip.
Soon again it'll start prancing, believe me it
knows how to skip
All around at night, this wondrous lonely beast.
If it overheats, please do come back with your
receipt!

And one last thing, old chap, it runs on water
and food,
So please give it some carrots, as for the elf,
some wood will do.

It will excrete the remnants at night, out the
reindeers end.
Enjoy your new toy, enjoy your new friend.'

Blue Crayfish

Tears of happiness, tears of joy,
The passionate cries of desperate boys,
That very essence creates a fish of royal blue.
One whose shell is sediment in being platonic
glue.

A Decapod hidden in a society of queers,
Orange, green and purple peers.
Layered in the thickness of agonistic intuition,
Spits at ignorance; naïveté and burns his own
innocence.

The most loyal of creatures; a blue, igneous
heart,
Oh the most leechless tie, a gordion knot you
shouldn't part,
The kindest of souls, ever shedding, never
ending,
Oh how foolish the Croatian leeches are for
unfriending.

Indeed you would be honoured to know the
wonder.
No ability for falseness, heartfelt bluntness
without blunder.

Therefore I plead for you to grate into your life:
Joy from the royal blue crayfish of moral friend,
sibling and wife.

Bagged Crickets

Has curiosity ever enticed you to look into
theatre masks?
Why the infamous symbol is two faces both
hidden with different pasts?
Like a coin perhaps, it's mutant and rich, with
two contrasting expressions:
Meet The Bagged Crickets of Theatre, a radiant
group of many mentions.

Bagged Crickets are repulsive, they're anatomy
just disgust,
Do I want to explain it? Should it remain never
discussed?
Alright, if you must know, either end of the body
sits a head,
Both connected to the stomach, diarrhoea spews
out of both ends.

Either mouth leaks faeces behind the closed
curtain,
They converse in dark wooden crevices, and the
truth cannot be certain,
As either head tells a story, both completely
different to the last,

Their mushy, internal security caused them to
vomit all forms of stories in the past.

They try to be everyone's friend! But inside they
hide their thoughts,
One face is more truthful, but which one? That
must be sought.
For you, unfortunately must discover for
yourself,
Which head on a bagged cricket is not leaking
faeces off the shelf.

Bodilised

I do think it's time we embraced our skills in
creation,
For you see, as human beings, we crafted every
nation
And language, and verb and the sort.
We invented every number, fraction and naught.

So I'm going to do the same, give a justice to a
sanction,
Construct and form a word to describe a specific
action.
This situation feels wrong, but of course things
do happen.
Life is unpredictable, but if you can, halt this
pattern.

For there is an act that some people do.
Accidental on occasion, but intentional too.
Humans are wired with lust, and when put
together they intertwine,
Feeding off the sweet juices of each others
bodily vine.

But with lust comes love! And sometimes
together they arrive.

Two people enjoy their savoury fruits and
romance begins to rise!
And thus they fall in love, oh how wonderful in
sweet.
This should be the way a lovely couple comes to
meet.

Of course there are times where love doesn't
grow,
The juices are enjoyably licked from lust alone.
And this, of course, is fine! No harm in a little
fun.
It only becomes an issue when the following is
done...

Some people promise romance, or exchange acts
of love,
They build a connection based the hearts above,
And while not official, feelings begin to emerge!
But in only one of them do the feelings actually
surge.

For this, I call it Bodilised, allow me to give
elaboration:
When someone is romantic but only wants
gratification,
They exchange sweet juice along the vine, and
one of them starts to feel,

And that one is left broken, just another body
left to heal.

Unrequited love is an act that of course will
always occur.
Two people will mate and the love lines begin to
blur,
But Bodilising is intentional, it's misleading to
the next.
You talk romantically to someone, but in the end
you just want sex.

You reduce them to merely a body, a number to
the count,
If this is your goal then say you just want to
increase your amount,
Don't hurt poor people like this, we understand
it does occur!
But if you know your making bodies, tell them
so they aren't hurt.

Bodilise: To diminish someone to merely a
number on a sexual scale (known as someone's
Body Count) while misleading said person with
romantic interest.

A Splitting with Zero Corners

Irony is tying but can also cause a split,
And it's ironic how Split led to such a split.

For a shoal of fish to flourish, there must be 16
corners,
No platonic leech of selfishness, no bagged
crickets or platonic hoarders.

Relationships are to fail if the 16 corners aren't
met,
The group will be left a baby blue, suffocated,
choked, upset.
You must be willing to embrace every members
flaws,
Their worrying gills, stubborn fins, mentally
painful claws.

Platonic leeches are most vile, their draining
nature is filled with discomfort too,
For surrounding yourself with selfless people is
the most selfish thing a leech can do.
So, platonic leeches, I urge you to return the
friendship I gave so soon,
You changed the status, now give my energy
back, it doesn't belong to you.

For the half of us mistreated and abandoned, I
promise soon our mental anguish will end,
As for the other half, I hope you're happy with
the outcome you created, so don't keep the split
waiting, friends...

My 19th Compulsion: String for Fought

This era comes to close, a new cycle will begin,
This year gave me experience I'd never thought
to see within
My inexperienced soul of life's eternal tune,
I am only 18... and has it really been 6 months
since June?

The next step is mysterious but descisions just
soon be made,
As I said once before, indecision is indeed a
plague,
And where I go from here will come as a
surprise,
Life sure has more in store than 17 year old me
realised.

I still have attachments, strings which won't cut,
As much as I can try, life has sewn them to my
gut,
But I'm trying to debate whether these subcious
ropes
Are what indeed is holding me back making
future tropes?

What do I need to release? And what do I need to clasp?
There's so much for me to learn in life's enteral class.
For I must fight off that which no longer serves
And embrace the next year opportunity, love and verse!

Fairwell, my dear readers, I hope the roller foster wasn't too violent,
If this was my first adult year, I hope the others are more violet,
But life has many colours, and only a few I've had the pleasure to taste,
Let's move onto the next step together, find the positives in whatever the future makes.

Every opportunity laced in indecision is merely a good dilemma in disguise, embrace it, and do what's right. There's no wrong answers, you'll feel the love in your gut and yours alone. Whatever the nibbling question is, it's there because you care. Your future will be bright regardless! So do what's right for you, fellow reader. Do what makes the universe sing peacefully to you.

9 789358 314823